Hetty Einzig

took a degree in modern languages and European drama and a
postgraduate degree in history of art. She worked first in the art
world, then as a journalist and author writing about health and
alternative therapies before training as a counsellor with the
Psychosynthesis & Education Trust.

Over the last eight years she has combined a private practice with
her work as Research Director of the Artemis Trust, a charity that
supports counselling and psychotherapy; this has included research,
writing and project development most particularly in the fields of
counselling in primary care and parenting education and support.

She is the author of two other BAC booklets, *Counselling &
Psychotherapy: Is it for me?* and *Personal Problems at Work -
Counselling as a Resource for the Manager* and lives in London
with her husband and two young daughters.

Becoming a

Counsellor

A Guide to Training in Counselling & Psychotherapy

Hetty Einzig

British Association for Counselling
1 Regent Place • Rugby • Warwickshire CV21 2PJ
Office 01788 550899 • Information Line 01788 578328 • Fax 01788 562189

© *BAC 1994*

ISBN 0 946181 36 5

Cover illustration by **Vicky Poles**

Produced by **British Association for Counselling, June 1994**
1 Regent Place, Rugby, Warwickshire CV21 2PJ
Company limited by guarantee 2175320 registered in England & Wales
Registered Charity 298361

Printed by Bourne Press Ltd.
3-11 Spring Road, Bournemouth BH1 4QA

Foreword

A large number of people are becoming aware that counselling is a valuable tool in maintaining the mental health of the nation. They are, therefore, seeking training either with a view to becoming counsellors or psychotherapists or to using counselling skills as part of their present role.

There is a wide range of training in counselling and psychotherapy available from short introductory courses through to Master and PhD degrees. This book sets out to explain the differences in the courses available and the areas in which the training obtained could be used. It provides the basic information to enable prospective students to start the search for appropriate training for their situation.

The spur to write this booklet has come from the many enquiries received from people setting out on this quest. Hetty Einzig has used her experience and that of colleagues and staff at BAC to answer the questions most frequently raised. She has a down to earth approach to a subject which can be quite bewildering.

Counselling is all about making your own decisions. This book will help you to make the first one in this direction.

Isobel Palmer
BAC Information & Publications Manager

Becoming a Counsellor
A Guide to Training in
Counselling & Psychotherapy

This booklet is intended to offer some answers to people who want advice on becoming a counsellor or psychotherapist, or using counselling as part of their job. Counselling is a rapidly developing profession and details of trainings, costs, accreditation and registration will change and should be checked with the individual training organisation.

If, after reading this booklet, you want to know more, there is a list of useful organisations and books which might be helpful at the end of the booklet. BAC publishes a directory, Training in Counselling & Psychotherapy, containing a wealth of information for people starting the search for training and which lists many of the courses available in this country. Other booklets and leaflets about careers in counselling are also obtainable.

If you are hoping to become a counsellor or to develop counselling skills, you will need to assess yourself honestly and accurately. An important dimension of this is becoming aware of the attitudes of others towards you. Self-assessment can be achieved by introspection and it will be a significant part of your counselling training. You may also decide perhaps to seek counselling or even psychotherapy for yourself. It is important to be clear why you need to help others as a counsellor. Anthony Storr in *The Art of Psychotherapy*, says that 'as a therapist, the more you learn about yourself the more you will be able to understand your clients; the more you learn about your clients the more you will be able to understand yourself'.

How do I want to be involved?

The whole field of counselling and psychotherapy is a relatively new one in Britain and the structure of it is emerging slowly. Here is an overview of the different ways in which people can be involved in the field. Like any such overall picture it is guilty of generalisation.

One way of being involved is, of course, as a client. If you want more information about being a client then we suggest you read BAC's booklet *Counselling & Psychotherapy: Is it for me?* The other usual ways of being involved in the counselling and psychotherapy field are:

1. As a user of counselling skills either
    a)   as part of a paid job or
    b)   in a voluntary capacity
2. As a counsellor
3. As a psychotherapist
4. As a participant in a personal growth programme.

To begin with it's helpful to get some sense of the range of training and experience which these categories cover. At one extreme a user of counselling skills might have done a day or two's training and be putting in a couple of hours a week using their skills on a telephone helpline. At the other extreme, a psychotherapist may have spent eight years in training and as many years of personal therapy and have been earning a living from practising as a full time psychotherapist for 20 years.

In other words, the levels of training and experience in the field can easily vary by as much as 200 to 1. At one end is someone who has done the equivalent of a first aid course and at the other end the equivalent of an experienced surgeon. We make no judgement as to the level of effectiveness of the user of counselling skills versus the experienced psychotherapist – in the right circumstances a first-aider can do as effective a job as the surgeon; sometimes more so.

1a) Using counselling skills as part of a paid job

There are a large number of jobs, particularly in the caring professions, where counselling skills enhance the relationships between the professionals and the people they deal with, e.g. nurses, teachers, GPs, carers, social workers. These people may use counselling skills as one part (often only a small part) of their job in an integrated and often unaware way. For example, a nurse may listen to patients and encourage them to talk about their feelings without any conscious thought of 'oh, now I must use my counselling skills to help them explore their feelings about their illness'.

The most basic counselling skill is to learn how to listen to another person in a non-judgemental, accepting and empathic way – a much harder skill to learn than it might seem! More advanced counselling skills include asking open-ended questions, helping someone to clarify their thoughts, feelings, goals, and so on. There is a large degree of overlap with 'interpersonal relationship skills' or 'communication skills'.

Many roles in organisations would be enhanced by a knowledge of counselling and it might be agreed that all 'managers', in the widest sense, should have basic counselling skills training. Good managers probably use these skills naturally but they can be even more effective with some training.

It is important for people using counselling skills to be aware of their limitations and know when it is necessary to refer on to someone trained to deal with the problems.

The number of people using counselling skills as part of their job certainly runs into hundreds of thousands – though the numbers who have been given adequate training in counselling skills is probably only a small proportion.

1b) Using counselling skills in voluntary work

Being voluntary does not in itself distinguish counselling skills from counselling. There are many voluntary counsellors. However, there are many organisations whose volunteer advice and support workers use counselling skills to a greater or lesser extent. These include well known national charities, such as the Samaritans, Victim Support and MIND, and local self-help groups such as cancer support groups, etc., which will most likely be affiliated to the Council for Voluntary Service.

The range of counselling skills used in voluntary organisations varies widely and may include, for example,
- the advice worker at the Citizen's Advice Bureau who will find many occasions when counselling skills will be needed as well as the provision of information.
- the Samaritan who listens – helpline workers need special training in telephone counselling skills

Many of the national organisations have their own training programmes but local groups are more likely to sponsor their volunteers on local counselling skills courses. Often people who have attended courses on their own initiative will be keen to offer their services as volunteers and can find local organisations who can use and further develop their skills.

Voluntary users of counselling skills use the same broad range of skills as those in category 1. Those offering support in self-help groups may not be aware that they are using counselling skills, and so, without the right training and support, may become exhausted and drop out. If you are a part of, or plan to set up, a self-help group, it is well worth gaining appropriate training and support for yourself.

The numbers of people using counselling skills on a voluntary basis runs into tens of thousands.

2. Counsellors

There has been a rapid growth in the numbers of counsellors as counselling has become more acceptable (through coverage in the media and more people talking about their own experiences). Counsellors are found in a variety of settings, education, medicine, industry and commerce, the church, and the voluntary sector. Often counsellors have a background within these areas. For instance: a student counsellor may well have been a college lecturer or teacher; a counsellor in general practice is often also a nurse; and in-company counsellors may have worked as personnel or welfare officers or occupational nurses. It is a great advantage to have inside knowledge of how the organisation functions although it is not essential.

There are many counsellors in the voluntary sector, often having been trained specially in the area of work undertaken by a specific charity, e.g. Relate, Victim Support, Cruse, Alcohol Concern and many others.

Counsellors may be full or part time. Frequently, counsellors in part time employment will also take clients in private practice. Whether full or part time, paid or voluntary, the standards required are the same, as laid down in the Code of Ethics & Practice for Counsellors for BAC members.

Some counsellors build on existing specialist knowledge to work with clients with particular problems (e.g. those with HIV or dependent on alcohol), others deal with a wide variety of age ranges and presenting problems.

Counselling can be long or short term; sometimes only one or two sessions, quite frequently 6 – 10 or even once weekly over a year or two. Some counsellors work full time (in centres or private practice) and rely on it for their income. Others are part time or voluntary, doing a few hours a week (e.g. for a specialist cancer clinic).

3. Psychotherapists

The distinction between counselling and psychotherapy is not a clear one as there is a lot of overlap between the kind of work they both do. You will find a more detailed description of the work in the BAC booklet *Counselling & Psychotherapy: Is it for me?*

Psychotherapists also work in a variety of settings. Examples: private and NHS clinics, hospitals, health centres, alternative medical centres, GP surgeries, psychotherapy training institutes, etc.

Some psychotherapists do 'brief' work (which can require a specialised training), offering say 6 – 12 sessions, some see clients once weekly for a year or two and some see clients several times a week for several years. Much depends on their style of working and the needs and means of the client.

There is some NHS provision of psychotherapy. However, it is difficult to work in the NHS as a psychotherapist unless you have an initial training in either psychiatry, clinical psychology or child psychotherapy. There are few voluntary psychotherapists – probably because of the costs and time involved in completing training.

At present there are about 70 member organisations of the UK Council for Psychotherapy (UKCP) which has established a Register for psychotherapists.

4. Participants / leaders in 'personal growth' programmes

The term 'personal growth' covers a variety of activities in groups or workshops such as assertiveness training, stress management, self-exploration workshops, art therapy, etc. Many of these are available as part of adult education programmes in colleges, churches or private training centres. Some people will have had the opportunity to attend personal development training through their jobs.

This type of groupwork is often the first taste anyone has of counselling skills from which an interest in further training develops. The term 'personal growth' is a bit odd but it's the best we have!

What you need to become a counsellor

Competence in the practice of counselling skills, counselling and psychotherapy depends on the following:
- Knowledge of theory
- Grasp of practical skills
- Specific personal qualities

A number of different activities contribute to the development of the above:
- Training courses
- Experience in 'client contact' situations
- Supervision (reviewing what you have covered during client contact with a more experienced practitioner or your peers)
- Personal Therapy (with you as the client – whether one to one or in a group).

How do these various elements interrelate?

Theory

There are a number of different 'schools' of counselling and psycho-therapy (Freudian, Jungian, Transactional Analysis, Person-Centred, Cognitive, Behavioural, Gestalt, Psychosynthesis, etc). Each has its own theory which provides a description of:

- how a human being 'works' psychologically.
- the process of psychological development in childhood and how the individual personality develops.

Theory can be learned in formal lectures, discussions, by studying textbooks and by essay writing, though the practical application of it demands opportunities to identify how theory is manifested in behaviour.

The individual's understanding of theory is not as important at counselling skills level, but is more important when practising counselling and psychotherapy. However, research evidence suggests that even at the most advanced levels of psychotherapy knowledge of theory is insufficient on its own, if the therapist does not possess the necessary personal qualities and practical competence and skill.

Skills

Counselling and psychotherapy demand a grasp of certain identifiable skills: e.g. listening, clarifying, helping the client to deepen contact with their feelings, ideas and memories, challenging the client.

Different schools have different views on what constitutes the necessary range of skills and on their relative importance but there is considerable agreement on core skills.

The skills are best learned experientially. Typically, during early training a tutor demonstrates a skill and the students do exercises practising the skill with each other – giving and receiving feedback on how well they do it. In later stages of training, additional opportunities to develop skills are provided by supervision, 'groupwork', and sessions reviewing experience with clients. Some courses encourage students to video or audio tape sessions for detailed feedback to the trainee.

Skills underpin all practice.

Qualities

It is widely believed that specific 'personal qualities' possessed by the counsellor or therapist are the most important factor in determining how effective the relationship is. These personal qualities are sometimes spoken of as 'attitudes', 'personal style' or something similar.

The key qualities are not easy to define. One description (based upon some excellent research) lays importance on the counsellor/therapist showing qualities of **empathy**, **acceptance** and **congruence**.

Empathy is 'putting yourself in the other person's shoes' in the deepest possible way and so experiencing their feelings and their understanding of the world. **Acceptance** results from essentially being non-judgemental, caring and supportive. **Congruence** is the practitioner's ability and willingness to express what they are really thinking and feeling when with the client rather than 'pretending' (as we may often do in a social or work setting). Other descriptive words which are sometimes used to describe these key qualities include *authenticity, respect, unconditional positive regard* and *caring*.

Personal qualities may play a slightly less active role in some schools than others. For example, traditional psychoanalytic psychotherapists are likely to reveal less of themselves than a 'person centred' or humanistic counsellor/therapist. However, the key qualities are recognised as being vital to any form of counselling and psychotherapy.

It is almost impossible directly to train someone to develop the required personal qualities. However, the qualities can be developed indirectly in a number of ways:
- via skills training. For example, the tutor and fellow students can give feedback on the level of congruence demonstrated by the student during an exercise in pairs.
- in theory and skills training by the tutor 'modelling' the qualities in their own interaction with students.
- in groupwork. Groupwork forms a significant part of the best training courses. It provides an opportunity for students to practise the skills they are learning by direct interaction with each other in a group setting. Groupwork provides an excellent opportunity to develop the requisite qualities in oneself, to receive personal feedback and to observe a lot of 'modelling' of the qualities (good and not so good) by fellow students.

- in personal therapy – with you as client. Again you would pick up, consciously and unconsciously, on the modelling of qualities by your therapist/counsellor. But most importantly, it is crucial to explore and work through your own deep feelings or issues. For example, a counsellor or therapist may not be able to empathise with a client's anger if they themselves are unwilling to contact and acknowledge their own anger. Only by doing sufficient work in personal therapy on their own issues around anger will they be able to raise their level of empathy in this situation.
- in client experience combined with supervision. For example, a counsellor with sexual inhibitions may describe their own embarrassment in dealing with a client talking about their sexual difficulties. In terms of personal qualities this would probably mean a diminished level of empathy and a lack of congruence in responding to the client. Talking about their embarrassment with peers or a supervisor (who may well share the embarrassment) can help the counsellor to face and deal with such issues with more ease.

The Value System

A number of people use skills which are of the same kind as 'counselling skills'. For example, managers, salespersons, customer service personnel, airline staff, leisure industry staff and many others are taught 'listening skills' or 'personal relationship skills' or 'communication skills' – all of which have much in common with counselling skills (they are derived from common research over the past 50 years or so).

In the same way, some of the personal qualities which contribute so much to counselling or therapy are also important in other jobs. For example, the customer service manager may say 'Send George out to see them – he's a sympathetic bloke and will calm them down'.

How, then, does the utilisation of the skills or personal qualities differ in the case of a counsellor from that of other jobs? In part the difference lies in the relative importance of the skills or personal qualities to the performance of the job – in counselling or therapy they are a very large part of the job indeed whereas in other jobs they are likely to be only a (small) part. But a more important difference usually lies in the value system underlying the job.

For example, a salesperson using empathy and listening skills with a potential customer is operating within a different value system from that adopted by a counsellor. The aim is to sell a car and the value system permits the utilisation of empathy and listening skills to the fullest in order to help make the sale. The counsellor/therapist on the other hand, operates within a value system which advocates helping the client with their life problems without exploiting them in any way (e.g. making a friend of the client in order to borrow money from them or get sexual favours from them, or even to assuage their loneliness). The salesperson might be able to demonstrate a high quality of empathy and excellent listening skills – but would make an extremely bad counsellor if the value system from selling were to be carried over into counselling.

Pre-Entry Requirements & Selection for Training

There are many introductory or basic counselling courses available lasting a few weeks or maybe even a year and for which there is no entry requirement.

Such a course will help you decide if you want to go on to more serious training. Many certificate and diploma courses ask for previous experience, such as relevant degrees in social work, teaching, etc., experience in the helping professions or completion of the introductory course.

The way this process works is not very consistent: for example a medical degree does not really have much to do with the practice of counselling and therapy and a psychology degree provides some valuable grounding in theory but no grounding in the qualities or skills which we regard as being more important. And a nurse or social worker may or may not have much experience of the exercise of counselling skills, depending on the particular setting where they have been working. Life experience or voluntary work in the counselling field may be more relevant.

Many organisations which offer counsellor training interview applicants. The nature of those interviews varies considerably and, if you decide to apply for training, you should ask about the criteria that interviewers will be applying to applicants. In some cases these interviews can take the form of a selection day. For example, Relate adopts a more elaborate procedure. Candidates are seen by officers of the local Relate Centre and, if thought suitable, go forward to a day-long selection conference conducted by the National organisation. During such conferences, group activities and two individual interviews are used to explore applicants' personal qualities (see page 9). Relate does not specify any particular academic requirements though it looks for people who can cope with its intensive residential training courses.

Don't be discouraged if you don't have the relevant qualifications for a particular organisation. Get the prospectuses for several trainings and look around for one that suits you.

Length of Training

Tables of typical course contents and the realistic aims that can be achieved in a variety of time units are given in the BAC publication *In-House & Tailor-Made Counselling Skills Training*.

Workshops (Half to One Day) and Short Courses (2 – 3 days)

These can fulfil a number of purposes.

1. They can act as an introduction to a subject or a basic understanding of what you can do with counselling skills.
2. They can be experiential – giving participants practical experience using role-play, etc.
3. They can provide specific information and expertise from which 'old hands' will benefit.
4. They can be groups where information and experience is exchanged.

It is important when choosing this type of training to obtain details of the level at which it will be pitched.

Introductory Courses

There is now an abundance of extended courses on a part-time basis. They may cover a period of 6 – 30 weeks (1 –- 3 academic terms) totalling 20 – 100 hours. These courses give people the opportunity to find out what counselling skills are all about.

These can be helpful for people in managerial roles and part of the job users, including volunteer workers in advice and support roles. Many of the latter receive in-house training in exchange for a commitment to the service.

Counselling Skills Courses

These will be 100 – 250 hours part-time and aimed at people using counselling skills as part of their job or as a step to full counsellor training. You should expect both theory and skills on these courses. A course of less than 150 hours would not fit one to work as a counsellor.

Counsellor Training

Courses of 250 hours and over are considered necessary for a fully trained counsellor. Such courses are usually part-time but there are a significant number of one year full-time courses available. Training aimed at preparing people to work as counsellors should include theory, a substantial practical bias, an opportunity to explore how your own life experience might affect your work as a counsellor and some supervised practice.

NB: BAC Accreditation requires 450 hours of training made up of 200 hours skills development and 250 hours of theory as well as 450 hours supervised practice.

Psychotherapy

Again, there is great variation in the length of psychotherapy training courses. In general, psychotherapy trainings are anything from 800 – 2,000 hours spread over 3 – 5 years part-time, or as a two year postgraduate training in addition to a three year counselling training. UKCP suggest that a psychotherapy training should have a minimum of 540 hours of theory over three years plus supervision, client contact hours and approximately four years personal therapy, bringing the average training up to about five years.

There are now a number of Masters courses at universities in counselling and psychotherapy.

Starting from scratch and going all the way with first a counselling skills course, followed by a counselling course and then a counselling/ psychotherapy Masters training would probably take seven years or more part-time.

Cost of Training

Counselling Skills

A basic counselling skills course at an Adult Education Institute typically costs £50-60 for about 20 hours. Often basic training in listening skills is free, if you offer your services to a helpline or support group. Taking such training implies commitment to some amount of unpaid voluntary service.

More advanced training in counselling skills at a private organisation can cost from £500-1,000. The cost may be less at a college or university. Of course, quality can be variable and the experiential content of the course may be less in an academic institution.

Counselling

A substantial counselling training would probably cost approximately £3-4,000. Then you would need to add up to £1,000 for supervision. Some trainings require personal therapy throughout or during the later stages which can add a further £500-2,000. In total, training to reach BAC accreditation standard is likely to cost about £5-6,000 spread over a three year period.

Counselling training to somewhat lower standard can be proportionately cheaper, i.e. a qualification offering 150 hours of training against the 450 hours required for BAC accreditation might cost only £1,300 in total.

The Relate counsellor training, comprising the acquisition of theory skills, couple casework and supervision amounting to 737 hours over two and a half years) is provided free if the trainee is sponsored by their local branch of Relate and with a commitment to give several hours a week voluntarily for a number of years.

Psychotherapy

Psychotherapy training starts at perhaps £2,500 and can be a lot more. Most courses require supervision and personal therapy in addition to the cost of the training. This will substantially increase the total costs. A 2 – 3 year postgraduate psychotherapy training might start at £1,500 per year plus supervision and therapy costs. The likelihood is that a full psychotherapy training will cost you between £10,000 and £20,000.

Grants & Scholarships

As far as we know there are few grants or scholarships offered by the training institutes. Many people (e.g. nurses, social workers) may be able to get their employers to pay for at least part of their training. The general picture is that it is easier to get training and supervision free or subsidised for initial training and gets harder for accreditable training.

BAC Educational Bursaries are available to those students wishing to attend a BAC Recognised Counsellor Training Course.

Income

Many counsellors and users of counselling skills are voluntary and unpaid.

Some of those who are paid see it as supplementary income, others as a full time job.

Fee rates are typically around £20-35 per session for a fully qualified and experienced counsellor. For up to date details of private practice fees, see the *Counselling & Psychotherapy Resources Directory* published by BAC. It is unusual for a counsellor or therapist to work with clients for more than 25 hours a week. Many do less. The Association for Student Counselling Advisory Service to Institutions recommends that counsellors spend no more than 16 – 20 hours per week in face to face counselling due to the stressful nature of the job.

Counsellors in training earn perhaps £10 per hour. A therapist at the top of his/her profession can charge £40 or more per session. It can take several years to build a client list.

There are some paid jobs in local counselling centres and increasingly as part of the GP team or in Social Services, with the advent of the Children Act. A relatively small, though increasing, number of jobs occur in industry, as nurse counsellors or as student counsellors, etc. Competition tends to be fierce for salaried counselling jobs. Salaries are often linked to pay scales for other professionals in the organisation and depend on the training and experience of the counsellor. BAC accreditation is often used as a standard.

Accreditation & Recognition

Currently, if you wish to practise as a counsellor or therapist there is nothing to stop you doing so right away. You do not need to have any kind of qualification – you can have some cards printed tomorrow describing yourself as a counsellor or therapist and see clients immediately. Needless to say, *we do not endorse this*!

Many training organisations, institutes and membership organisations offer a certificate, diploma, 'membership of' or something similar. These systems of recognition are important as an attempt to protect the public, raise standards, provide the individual with some confirmation of their own competence and so on. There is currently no single system – rather there are well over 100 systems observing no common standards.

In the counselling area, BAC already has an accreditation system. Some other major national organisations (for example Relate, Cruse, etc) also have some form of certification or accreditation system which is widely recognised. It is probable that these systems will be brought together into a single comprehensive national system of registration for counsellors over the next few years.

In the psychotherapy area the UK Council for Psychotherapy (UKCP) has established a single national system of registration for psycho-therapists covering member organisations, as stated previously.

The British Psychological Society has also established a system of qualification in 'counselling psychology' (fitting alongside their existing Clinical Psychology qualification). To date BPS restrict membership to individuals with a first degree in psychology.

Much work is being done by BAC, UKCP and other counselling bodies to raise standards of training and practice. This includes work with the Department of Employment on NVQs and developing ties in Europe. It is important to keep abreast of developments which are reported in BAC's quarterly journal *Counselling,* which is available free to BAC members or can be bought by subscription.

There is a wide range of training on offer, from introductory courses through to Master degrees and PhDs. Certificates and diploma syllabuses are set by a number of bodies, details of which are given in *Training in Counselling & Psychotherapy* published annually by BAC.

The BAC Recognition of Courses Scheme in operation is for existing courses which have graduated at least one cohort of students and which has been able to develop in the light of that experience. The Scheme is not just a validation of course design. It looks at the delivery and assessment processes of a course as well. Further details are available from BAC.

If you are thinking of simply learning and utilising counselling skills you can probably afford not to worry about what kind of 'certificate' you get at the end of your training but concentrate on picking a training which offers an experiential component and develops skills and personal qualities.

If you are thinking of taking up counselling as a career then probably the best bet currently is to follow a path which will take you towards BAC accreditation (details of requirements available on request).

What Do I Want?

It is worth asking yourself a few questions at the outset. Am I aiming for a career as a counsellor/psychotherapist? Do I want a full time job or part time? Do I want to practise on a voluntary basis? Will this training help me in my job?

How sure am I that I want to do this sort of thing? If you have not had any experience of counselling/therapy we would suggest that you get some initial experience and see whether you like it – for instance by doing a basic counselling skills course. There are plenty of these introductory courses available and it is a good idea to get some experience in a voluntary capacity. Some organisations using voluntary counsellors, such as Samaritans, Cruse, Parent Network, etc., will provide basic counselling skills training.

Why do I really want to enter this field? Because I want to help other people, or because I want to look at myself and improve the quality of my own life? For most people entering this field both are true. Deciding how to enter the field and try it out is easier if you can be honest with yourself and recognise what you want for yourself.

Some counsellors/therapists come from quite damaged childhoods. This is by no means necessarily a disqualification – it can eventually be a powerful resource. But it is important to recognise the need to sort out your own problems too, so you do not substitute caring for others for attending to your own psychological and emotional needs.

How important is accreditation or registration? How important are the less tangible (and possibly more important) goals of status, recognition or affirmation of myself? What sort of work do I see myself doing in the long run? With whom do I wish to work? Some people are happy working with a small number of people very intensively over a period of a year or two. Others prefer to work with larger numbers of people less intensively over just a few weeks. Some people want to specialise in a particular field such as relationship counselling, counselling with issues of sexuality, bereavement work or working with children. Some want to work particularly with people with disabilities, disadvantages, severe disturbances, drug dependencies, or with other specialised groups of people.

Lastly, some practical questions. What funding can I afford? How much time do I have for training? How far am I prepared to travel for training? Where can I work to gain experience?

The Transition to a New Career

If you have decided that you want to work in the counselling or psychotherapy field then you are probably thinking in terms of making a transition from your existing career to a new one. In fact most people entering counselling or psychotherapy in Britain do so in their 30s or 40s as a second career. It is different in the USA. Many are initially unsure about whether they want to take up this work and enter fairly tentatively – trying out an initial course to get the flavour first.

Because of the problem of financing the training (and the cost of the supervision and personal therapy required as the training advances), and also because of the length of the training, most people have to make a long transition from their existing career to the new one.

For example, a nurse might do a counselling skills course and discover enjoyment in using the skills. As interest grows, a full counselling or psychotherapy training over 2 – 3 years can be arranged (if skilful an employer may be persuaded to pay for this training). As training progresses a few clients may be seen in off-duty hours – which helps pay for some supervision and the personal therapy – which is sometimes required as part of the training. If thoroughly gripped by the bug the decision might now be made to embark on a three year counselling diploma or two year psychotherapy masters training, seeing more clients in off-duty time both to gain more experience and help with finances and after a year of this to take the plunge and go part time. Finally, the nurse has become a highly qualified therapist relying on this as a full time income.

This kind of transition is, clearly, extremely demanding in time and money. It takes considerable dedication to complete between 5 and 7 years training at a cost in excess of £10,000.

Making a Start

If you have no experience in this field then we strongly suggest that you get some before going any further. There are a number of alternatives.

There are numerous introductory and basic counselling skills courses available in most areas at colleges, adult education centres or training institutes. These courses are usually experiential, giving a good taste of the skills necessary and some understanding of the personal involvement and commitment. BAC publishes a Directory, *Training in Counselling & Psychotherapy*, which lists all types of courses and has a useful preface to help you find the most appropriate training for your needs.

If you want to take your interest in counselling further, the tutors on your course will encourage you to get some experience. Some people attending the course will be sponsored by counselling organisations such as the local youth counselling service or self-help groups; such services are often looking for recruits. Others, such as Samaritans, Cruse, etc., provide their own basic training in counselling skills plus a few hours a week practising those skills. A good way to find out about groups looking for volunteer counsellors is to contact your local Council for Voluntary Services.

Another starting point might be to take an introductory course in Co-counselling and join a local group where you can practise with each other.

Once you are really sure this field is where you want to be then you can plunge straight into a full counselling or psychotherapy course (though some courses restrict entry to people who have some experience at the counselling skills level). The BAC Directory lists many counselling and psychotherapy courses and UKCP will send you a list of member organisations to contact for psychotherapy courses.

Choosing a Course

In the initial stages it is important to choose a course which is strong on the experiential content rather than on theory. It is a good idea to ask questions about what percentage of the time is spent on doing practical exercises and groupwork versus the amount of time spent in theory lectures, writing essays and studying. Beware particularly of the counselling skills courses which are actually a series of lectures, or those where the emphasis is on obtaining an academic qualification rather than using the skills at a practical level. Ask people in your local area for their personal experience and opinion of the courses available. BAC can provide a list of counsellors and therapists in your area whom you might contact, to discuss what is available. It is also very important that the course tutor has practised experience of using counselling skills or of being a counsellor or therapist. Satisfy yourself that this is true and do not be afraid to ask pertinent questions.

Whatever the claims for correspondence courses, they should only be viewed as an introduction to counselling. It is unlikely that they would contribute much to the training element for BAC individual accreditation. This is because they have little or no counselling practice under supervision and have little opportunity for observation and practice of counselling skills with feedback from both staff and fellow students, which are considered to be very important aspects of training. The better correspondence courses will have residential tutorials.

Deciding upon a 'school' of counselling or psychotherapy (Transactional Analysis, Person-Centred, Gestalt, etc.) is not all that relevant at the counselling skills level because theory is so much less important at this stage than personal qualities and skills. Entering at the counselling or psychotherapy level your choice will influence your training for two (or probably more) years. Of course, you can always change allegiances, but this is likely to mean starting again from scratch with the additional cost in time and money which this will involve. Hence it pays to shop around in making your initial choice. Many institutes offer introductory courses which give you a taster. Talking to practitioners can give you some kind of a feel for that school. A few sessions with a counsellor or therapist can also give you the flavour of a school. As far as possible choose a school which is reasonably compatible with you as a person. The books by Rowan and Dryden give some idea of the range available.

You will also want to bear in mind whether the course is Recognised by BAC or not, or whether the course offers a reputable diploma or certificate which could take you towards personal BAC accreditation. BAC training information and accreditation criteria can give a valuable insight here. Your choice at the counselling or therapy level may be partly determined by what time you have available for training (for example, some courses involve an evening a week, some a day a week, others a three day unit several times a year and others involve one weekend a month). The BAC Training Directory, National Section, gives details of courses with modular/residential components which may fit in better with your other commitments. What is available to you within travelling distance and lastly, of course, cost, will also play major parts in your decision.

Good luck!

Addresses

British Association for Counselling
1 Regent Place
Rugby CV21 2PJ
Info Line: 01788 578328
Office: 01788 550899
Fax: 01788 562189

UK Council for Psychotherapy (UKCP)
Regent's College
Inner Circle, Regent's Park,
London NW1 4NS
Tel: 0171-487 7554

Cruse
Cruse House
126 Sheen Road
Richmond
Surrey TW9 1UR
Tel: 0181-940 4818

Relate
Herbert Gray College
Little Church Street
Rugby CV21 3AP
Tel: 01788 573421

The Samaritans
17 Uxbridge Road
Slough SL1 1SN
Tel: 01753 24322

Books

Handbook of Counselling in Britain Ed. Windy Dryden, David Charles-Edwards & Ray Woolfe. Routledge 1989
Counselling in Action   Series covering all the main forms of counselling/psychotherapy. Series ed. Windy Dryden. Sage Publications 1990-91.
The Reality Game: A Guide to Humanistic Counselling & Therapy. John Rowan. Routledge 1983.
The Art of Psychotherapy Anthony Storr. Heinemann 1979
Introduction to Psychotherapy David Brown & Jonathan Pedder. Tavistock 1979
The Case for a Personal Psychotherapy P. Lomas. Oxford University Press 1981.
On Becoming a Psychotherapist Ed. Windy Dryden & Laurence Spurling. Tavistock/Routledge 1989
A Guide to Humanistic Psychology Pamphlet. Association of Humanistic Psychology, c/o The Gale Centre, Whitaker's Way, Loughton, Essex.
Training in Counselling & Psychotherapy – A Directory. BAC published annually (November)

Counselling & Psychotherapy Resources Directory
BAC published annually (January)
In-House & Tailor-Made Counselling Skills Training –
A Directory. BAC February 1993
Resource Pack for Volunteer Counsellors Ed. Nick Rans. BAC 1992
Counselling & Psychotherapy: Is it for me? Hetty Einzig. BAC
4th ed. 1993.
Personal Problems at Work   Hetty Einzig. BAC 1992.
Guide to Training Courses in Counselling Association for Student
Counselling in association with BAC, 1992 revised ed.
Recognition of Counsellor Training Courses BAC 1991

JOBFILE available on subscription from BAC
The BAC **Training Information Pack** is available from BAC – please
send A4 s.a.e.

*All those marked * obtainable mail order from BAC.*